National Preparedness Goal

First Edition
September 2011

Homeland Security

Table of Contents

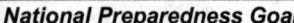

This page intentionally left blank.

Introduction

Presidential Policy Directive 8: National Preparedness (PPD-8) describes the Nation's approach to preparing for the threats and hazards that pose the greatest risk to the security of the United States. National preparedness is the shared responsibility of our whole community. Every member contributes, including individuals, communities, the private and nonprofit sectors, faith-based organizations, and Federal, state, and local[1] governments. We describe our security and resilience posture through the core capabilities (see Table 1) that are necessary to deal with great risks, and we will use an integrated, layered, and all-of-Nation approach as our foundation. We define success as:

> A secure and resilient Nation with the capabilities required across the whole community to prevent, protect against, mitigate, respond to, and recover from the threats and hazards that pose the greatest risk.

Using the core capabilities, we achieve the National Preparedness Goal by:

- Preventing, avoiding, or stopping a threatened or an actual act of terrorism.

- Protecting our citizens, residents, visitors, and assets against the greatest threats and hazards in a manner that allows our interests, aspirations, and way of life to thrive.

- Mitigating the loss of life and property by lessening the impact of future disasters.

- Responding quickly to save lives, protect property and the environment, and meet basic human needs in the aftermath of a catastrophic incident.

- Recovering through a focus on the timely restoration, strengthening, and revitalization of infrastructure, housing, and a sustainable economy, as well as the health, social, cultural, historic, and environmental fabric of communities affected by a catastrophic incident.

The core capabilities contained in the Goal are the distinct critical elements necessary for our success. They are highly interdependent and will require us to use existing preparedness networks and activities, improve training and exercise programs, promote innovation, and ensure that the administrative, finance, and logistics systems are in place to support these capabilities. The capability targets[2]—the performance threshold(s) for each core capability—will guide our allocation of resources in support of our national preparedness.

Individual and community preparedness is fundamental to our success. By providing the necessary knowledge and skills, we seek to enable the whole community to contribute to and benefit from national preparedness. This includes children, individuals with disabilities and others with access and functional needs, diverse communities, and people with limited English proficiency. Their needs and contributions must be integrated into our efforts. Each community contributes to the Goal and strengthens our national preparedness by preparing for the risks that are most relevant and urgent for them individually.

We have made great progress in building and sustaining our national preparedness. The Goal builds on these achievements, but our aspirations must be even higher to match the greatest risks facing our Nation. As we prepare for these challenges, our core capabilities will evolve to meet those challenges.

---

[1] For the purposes of this document, "state and local" includes tribal and territorial governments.

[2] The capability targets will serve as the basis for the development of performance measures to track our progress.

Core Capabilities

Overview

Core capabilities are essential for the execution of each of the five mission areas: Prevention, Protection, Mitigation, Response, and Recovery (see Table 1). To assess both our capacity and our gaps, each core capability includes capability targets for which measures will be developed. The core capabilities and capability targets are not exclusive to any single level of government or organization, but rather require the combined efforts of the whole community.

Table 1: Core Capabilities by Mission Area[3]

Prevention	Protection	Mitigation	Response	Recovery
Planning				
Public Information and Warning				
Operational Coordination				
Forensics and Attribution	Access Control and Identity Verification	Community Resilience	Critical Transportation	Economic Recovery
Intelligence and Information Sharing	Cybersecurity	Long-term Vulnerability Reduction	Environmental Response/Health and Safety	Health and Social Services
Interdiction and Disruption	Intelligence and Information Sharing	Risk and Disaster Resilience Assessment	Fatality Management Services	Housing
Screening, Search, and Detection	Interdiction and Disruption	Threats and Hazard Identification	Infrastructure Systems	Infrastructure Systems
	Physical Protective Measures		Mass Care Services	Natural and Cultural Resources
	Risk Management for Protection Programs and Activities		Mass Search and Rescue Operations	
	Screening, Search, and Detection		On-scene Security and Protection	
	Supply Chain Integrity and Security		Operational Communications	
			Public and Private Services and Resources	
			Public Health and Medical Services	
			Situational Assessment	

---

[3] Planning, Public Information and Warning, and Operational Coordination are core capabilities common to all mission areas.

These five mission areas serve as an aid in organizing our national preparedness activities, and do not constrain or limit integration across mission areas and core capabilities, which by their nature are highly interdependent and applicable to any threat or hazard. These mission areas exist along a continuum, and there is a dynamic interplay between and among them and even some commonality in the core capabilities essential to each.

These core capabilities represent an evolution from the Target Capabilities List.[4] The transition to core capabilities expands the focus to include Mitigation and allows greater focus on Prevention and Protection activities based on experience since the release of Homeland Security Presidential Directive 8 (HSPD-8). The capability targets associated with these core capabilities are ambitious. *These are not targets for any single jurisdiction or agency; achieving these targets will require a national effort involving the whole community.* Each mission area relies on the whole community to ensure success. This includes children,[5] individuals with disabilities and others with access and functional needs, diverse communities, and people with limited English proficiency.

Three core capabilities span all five mission areas: Planning, Public Information and Warning, and Operational Coordination. These common core capabilities serve to unify the mission areas and, in many ways, are necessary for the success of the remaining core capabilities. Additionally, a number of core capabilities directly involve more than one mission area and are listed in each mission area as appropriate.

Core capabilities and targets, like the risks we face, are not static. They will be vetted and refined, taking into consideration the risk and resource requirements, during the planning process established through PPD-8.

Risk and the Core Capabilities

Understanding the greatest risks to the Nation's security and resilience is a critical step in identifying the core capabilities and capability targets. All levels of government and the whole community should present and assess risk in a similar manner to provide a common understanding of the threats and hazards confronting our Nation. The information gathered during a risk assessment also enables a prioritization of preparedness efforts and an ability to identify our capability requirements across the whole community.

In accordance with PPD-8, and in coordination with Federal departments and agencies, a Strategic National Risk Assessment was conducted.[6] The results of the assessment indicate that a wide range of threats and hazards pose a significant risk to the Nation, affirming the need for an all-hazards, capability-based approach to preparedness planning. Key findings include:

- Natural hazards, including hurricanes, earthquakes, tornados, wildfires, and floods, present a significant and varied risk across the country.

---

[4] For a crosswalk of the Target Capabilities List against the core capabilities, see http://www.fema.gov/ppd8.

[5] Children require a unique set of considerations across the core capabilities and capability targets contained within this document. It is strongly encouraged that this be taken into consideration as part of any integrated planning effort.

[6] The complete results of the Strategic National Risk Assessment are classified. For an unclassified summary, see http://www.fema.gov/ppd8.

- A virulent strain of pandemic influenza could kill hundreds of thousands of Americans, affect millions more, and result in economic loss. Additional human and animal infectious diseases, including those previously undiscovered, may present significant risks.

- Technological and accidental hazards, such as dam failures or chemical substance spills or releases, have the potential to cause extensive fatalities and severe economic impacts, and the likelihood of occurrence may increase due to aging infrastructure.

- Terrorist organizations or affiliates may seek to acquire, build, and use weapons of mass destruction (WMD). Conventional terrorist attacks, including those by "lone actors" employing explosives and armed attacks, present a continued risk to the Nation.

- Cyber attacks can have their own catastrophic consequences and can also initiate other hazards, such as power grid failures or financial system failures, which magnify the potential impact of cyber incidents.

These findings supported the development of the core capabilities, as well as the establishment of capability targets for the Goal. Additionally, the Response and Recovery mission areas go one step further by focusing on a set of core capabilities based on the impact of a no-notice, cascading incident. Such an incident would likely stress the abilities of our Nation. A set of planning factors, drawing across three hazards identified by the Strategic National Risk Assessment (i.e., a large-scale earthquake, a major hurricane, and a WMD attack), were developed to mimic this cascading incident and identify the necessary core capabilities. The specific findings and the planning factors for the cascading incident results will be revisited as part of the recurring update of the Strategic National Risk Assessment.

Mission Area: Prevention

Prevention includes those capabilities necessary to avoid, prevent, or stop a threatened or actual act of terrorism.[7] It is focused on ensuring we are optimally prepared to prevent an imminent terrorist attack within the United States.

Preventing an *imminent* terrorist threat to the homeland will require Prevention core capabilities. In addition, it will trigger a robust and collaborative investigative process.[8] Prevention also includes the intelligence, law enforcement, and homeland defense activities conducted in the event of an act of terrorism in the homeland to determine if follow-on attacks are planned and to thwart and/or apprehend the adversary.

The terrorist threat is dynamic and complex and combating it is not the sole responsibility of a single entity or community. Ensuring the security of the homeland requires the execution of terrorism prevention through extensive collaboration with government and nongovernmental entities, international partners, and the private sector. We will foster a rapid, coordinated, all-of-Nation, effective terrorism prevention effort that reflects the full range of capabilities critical to avoid, prevent, or stop a threatened or actual act of terrorism in the homeland.

---

[7] Unlike other mission areas which are all-hazards by design, PPD-8 specifically focuses Prevention-related activities on an imminent terrorist threat.

[8] An investigative process is the systematic collection and analysis of information pertaining to factors suspected of being, contributing to, or having caused a terrorism threat or a terrorism incident. A well-conducted process will routinely leverage multiple core capabilities to accomplish its purpose in a holistic, all-of-Nation approach.

Table 2: Prevention Mission Area Capabilities and Preliminary Targets[9]

Prevention Mission Area Capabilities and Preliminary Targets	
Planning	Conduct a systematic process engaging the whole community as appropriate in the development of executable strategic, operational, and/or community-based approaches to meet defined objectives.

1. Identify critical objectives based on the planning requirement, provide a complete and integrated picture of the sequence and scope of the tasks to achieve the objectives, and ensure the objectives are implementable within the time frame contemplated within the plan using available resources for prevention-related plans.
2. Develop and execute appropriate courses of action in coordination with Federal, state, local, and private sector entities in order to prevent an imminent terrorist attack within the United States.

Public Information and Warning	Deliver coordinated, prompt, reliable, and actionable information to the whole community through the use of clear, consistent, accessible, and culturally and linguistically appropriate methods to effectively relay information regarding any threat or hazard, as well as the actions being taken and the assistance being made available, as appropriate.

1. Share prompt and actionable messages, to include National Terrorism Advisory System alerts, with the public and other stakeholders, as appropriate, to aid in the prevention of imminent or follow-on terrorist attacks, consistent with the timelines specified by existing processes and protocols.
2. Provide public awareness information to inform the general public on how to identify and provide terrorism-related information to the appropriate law enforcement authorities, thereby enabling the public to act as a force multiplier in the prevention of imminent or follow-on acts of terrorism.

Operational Coordination	Establish and maintain a unified and coordinated operational structure and process that appropriately integrates all critical stakeholders and supports the execution of core capabilities.

1. Execute operations with functional and integrated communications among appropriate entities to prevent initial or follow-on terrorist attacks within the United States in accordance with established protocols.

Forensics and Attribution	Conduct forensic analysis and attribute terrorist acts (including the means and methods of terrorism) to their source, to include forensic analysis as well as attribution for an attack and for the preparation for an attack in an effort to prevent initial or follow-on acts and/or swiftly develop counter-options.

1. Prioritize physical evidence collection and analysis to assist in preventing initial or follow-on terrorist acts.
2. Prioritize chemical, biological, radiological, nuclear, and explosive (CBRNE) material (bulk and trace) collection and analysis to assist in preventing initial or follow-on terrorist acts.
3. Prioritize biometric collection and analysis to assist in preventing initial or follow-on terrorist acts.
4. Prioritize digital media and network exploitation to assist in preventing initial or follow-on terrorist acts.

---

[9] The capability targets serve as strategic targets and will be vetted and refined, taking into consideration risk information and resource requirements, during the planning process established through PPD-8.

Prevention Mission Area Capabilities and Preliminary Targets	
Intelligence and Information Sharing	Provide timely, accurate, and actionable information resulting from the planning, direction, collection, exploitation, processing, analysis, production, dissemination, evaluation, and feedback of available information concerning threats to the United States, its people, property, or interests; the development, proliferation, or use of WMDs; or any other matter bearing on U.S. national or homeland security by Federal, state, local, and other stakeholders. Information sharing is the ability to exchange intelligence, information, data, or knowledge among Federal, state, local, or private sector entities, as appropriate.

1. Anticipate and identify emerging and/or imminent threats through the intelligence cycle.
2. Share relevant, timely, and actionable information and analysis with Federal, state, local, private sector, and international partners and develop and disseminate appropriate classified/unclassified products.
3. Ensure Federal, state, local, and private sector partners possess or have access to a mechanism to submit terrorism-related information and/or suspicious activity reports to law enforcement.

Interdiction and Disruption	Delay, divert, intercept, halt, apprehend, or secure threats and/or hazards.

1. Maximize our ability to interdict specific conveyances, cargo, and persons associated with an imminent terrorist threat or act in the land, air, and maritime domains to prevent entry into the United States or to prevent an incident from occurring in the Nation.
2. Conduct operations to render safe and dispose of CBRNE hazards in multiple locations and in all environments, consistent with established protocols.
3. Prevent terrorism financial/material support from reaching its target, consistent with established protocols.
4. Prevent terrorist acquisition of and the transfer of CBRNE materials, precursors, and related technology, consistent with established protocols.
5. Conduct tactical counterterrorism operations in multiple locations and in all environments, consistent with established protocols.

Screening, Search, and Detection	Identify, discover, or locate threats and/or hazards through active and passive surveillance and search procedures. This may include the use of systematic examinations and assessments, sensor technologies, or physical investigation and intelligence.

1. Maximize the screening of targeted cargo, conveyances, mail, baggage, and people associated with an imminent terrorist threat or act using technical, non-technical, intrusive, or non-intrusive means.
2. Initiate operations immediately to locate persons and networks associated with an imminent terrorist threat or act.
3. Conduct CBRNE search/detection operations in multiple locations and in all environments, consistent with established protocols.

Mission Area: Protection

Protection includes capabilities to safeguard the homeland against acts of terrorism and man-made or natural disasters. It is focused on actions to protect the citizens, residents, visitors, and critical assets, systems, and networks against the greatest risks to our Nation in a manner that allows our interests, aspirations, and way of life to thrive. We will create conditions for a safer, more secure, and more resilient Nation by enhancing Protection through cooperation and collaboration with all sectors of society.

The Protection capabilities are achieved through specific mission activities.[10] These include, but are not limited to, critical infrastructure protection,[11] cybersecurity,[12] border security, immigration security, protection of key leadership and events, maritime security, transportation security, defense of agriculture and food, defense against WMD threats, and health security.

Table 3: Protection Mission Area Capabilities and Preliminary Targets[13]

Protection Mission Area Capabilities and Preliminary Targets	
Planning	Conduct a systematic process engaging the whole community, as appropriate, in the development of executable strategic, operational, and/or community-based approaches to meet defined objectives.
1. Develop protection plans that identify critical objectives based on planning requirements, provide a complete and integrated picture of the sequence and scope of the tasks to achieve the planning objectives, and implement planning requirements within the time frame contemplated within the plan using available resources for protection-related plans. 2. Implement, exercise, and maintain plans to ensure continuity of operations.	
Public Information and Warning	Deliver coordinated, prompt, reliable, and actionable information to the whole community through the use of clear, consistent, accessible, and culturally and linguistically appropriate methods to effectively relay information regarding any threat or hazard and, as appropriate, the actions being taken and the assistance being made available.
1. Use effective and accessible indication and warning systems to communicate significant hazards to involved operators, security officials, and the public (including alerts, detection capabilities, and other necessary and appropriate assets).	
Operational Coordination	Establish and maintain a unified and coordinated operational structure and process that appropriately integrates all critical stakeholders and supports the execution of core capabilities.
1. Establish and maintain partnership structures among Protection elements to support networking, planning, and coordination.	
Access Control and Identity Verification	Apply a broad range of physical, technological, and cyber measures to control admittance to critical locations and systems, limiting access to authorized individuals to carry out legitimate activities.
1. Implement and maintain protocols to verify identity and authorize, grant, or deny physical and cyber access to specific locations, information, and networks.	

---

[10] We will describe how the capabilities support our efforts to achieve the mission activities in future products.
[11] See Critical Infrastructure in Appendix A for a full explanation.
[12] See Cybersecurity in Appendix A for an explanation of cybersecurity as both a mission activity and a core capability.
[13] The capability targets serve as strategic targets and will be vetted and refined, taking into consideration risk information and resource requirements, during the planning process established through PPD-8.

Protection Mission Area Capabilities and Preliminary Targets

Cybersecurity	Protect against damage to, the unauthorized use of, and/or the exploitation of (and, if needed, the restoration of) electronic communications systems and services (and the information contained therein).

1. Implement risk-informed guidelines, regulations, and standards to ensure the security, reliability, integrity, and availability of critical information, records, and communications systems and services through collaborative cybersecurity initiatives and efforts.
2. Implement and maintain procedures to detect malicious activity and to conduct technical and investigative-based countermeasures, mitigations, and operations against malicious actors to counter existing and emerging cyber-based threats, consistent with established protocols.

Intelligence and Information Sharing	Provide timely, accurate, and actionable information resulting from the planning, direction, collection, exploitation, processing, analysis, production, dissemination, evaluation, and feedback of available information concerning threats to the United States, its people, property, or interests; the development, proliferation, or use of WMDs; or any other matter bearing on U.S. national or homeland security by Federal, state, local, and other stakeholders. Information sharing is the ability to exchange intelligence, information, data, or knowledge among Federal, state, local or private sector entities as appropriate.

1. Anticipate and identify emerging and/or imminent threats through the intelligence cycle.
2. Share relevant, timely, and actionable information and analysis with Federal, state, local, private sector, and international partners and develop and disseminate appropriate classified/unclassified products.
3. Provide Federal, state, local, and private sector partners with or access to a mechanism to submit terrorism-related information and/or suspicious activity reports to law enforcement.

Interdiction and Disruption	Delay, divert, intercept, halt, apprehend, or secure threats and/or hazards.

1. Deter, detect, interdict, and protect against domestic and transnational criminal and terrorist activities that threaten the security of the homeland across key operational activities and critical infrastructure sectors.
2. Intercept the malicious movement and acquisition/transfer of CBRNE materials and related technologies.

Physical Protective Measures	Reduce or mitigate risks, including actions targeted at threats, vulnerabilities, and/or consequences, by controlling movement and protecting borders, critical infrastructure, and the homeland.

1. Implement and maintain risk-informed physical protections, countermeasures, and policies protecting people, structures, materials, products, and systems associated with key operational activities and critical infrastructure sectors.

Protection Mission Area Capabilities and Preliminary Targets	
Risk Management for Protection Programs and Activities	Identify, assess, and prioritize risks to inform Protection activities and investments.

1. Ensure critical infrastructure sectors and Protection elements have and maintain risk assessment processes to identify and prioritize assets, systems, networks, and functions.
2. Ensure operational activities and critical infrastructure sectors have and maintain appropriate threat, vulnerability, and consequence tools to identify and assess threats, vulnerabilities, and consequences.

Screening, Search, and Detection	Identify, discover, or locate threats and/or hazards through active and passive surveillance and search procedures. This may include the use of systematic examinations and assessments, sensor technologies, or physical investigation and intelligence.

1. Screen cargo, conveyances, mail, baggage, and people using information-based and physical screening technology and processes.
2. Detect WMD, traditional, and emerging threats and hazards of concern using:
   a. A laboratory diagnostic capability and the capacity for food, agricultural (plant/animal), environmental, medical products, and clinical samples
   b. Bio-surveillance systems
   c. CBRNE detection systems
   d. Trained healthcare, emergency medical, veterinary, and environmental laboratory professionals.

Supply Chain Integrity and Security	Strengthen the security and resilience of the supply chain.

1. Secure and make resilient key nodes, methods of transport between nodes, and materials in transit.

Mission Area: Mitigation

Mitigation includes those capabilities necessary to reduce loss of life and property by lessening the impact of disasters. It is focused on the premise that individuals, the private sector, communities, critical infrastructure, and the Nation as a whole are made more resilient when the consequences and impacts, the duration, and the financial and human costs to respond to and recover from adverse incidents are all reduced.

Given the draining impact of disasters and catastrophic incidents on the Nation, Mitigation stands as a critical linchpin to reduce or eliminate the long-term risks to life, property, and well-being. Without a change in our long-term planning, the Nation's risks and associated consequences will continue to escalate. Spanning across community planning, critical infrastructure, public health, and future land use, Mitigation requires an understanding of the threats and hazards that, in turn, feed into the assessment of risk and disaster resilience in the community. The whole community, therefore, has a role in risk reduction, by recognizing, understanding, communicating, and planning for a community's future resilience. Mitigation links the long-term activities of the whole community to reduce or eliminate the risk of threats and hazards developing into disasters and the impacts of the disasters that occur.

Although Mitigation is the responsibility of the whole community, a great deal of mitigation activity occurs at the local level. The assessment of risk and resilience must therefore begin at the community level and serve to inform our state, regional, and national planning. For risk information to result in specific risk reduction actions, leaders—whether elected in a jurisdiction, appointed in a given department, a nongovernmental director, a sector official, or in business or communities—must have the ability to recognize, understand, communicate, and plan for a community's future resilience. The establishment of trusted relationships among leaders in a community prior to a disaster can greatly reduce the risks to life, property, the natural environment, and well-being. When these leaders are prepared, the whole community matures and becomes better prepared to reduce the risks over the long term.

Table 4: Mitigation Mission Area Capabilities and Preliminary Targets[14]

Mitigation Mission Area Capabilities and Preliminary Targets	
Planning	Conduct a systematic process engaging the whole community as appropriate in the development of executable strategic, operational, and/or community-based approaches to meet defined objectives.
1. Develop approved hazard mitigation plans that address all relevant threats/hazards in accordance with the results of their risk assessment within all states and territories.	
Public Information and Warning	Deliver coordinated, prompt, reliable, and actionable information to the whole community through the use of clear, consistent, accessible, and culturally and linguistically appropriate methods to effectively relay information regarding any threat or hazard and, as appropriate, the actions being taken and the assistance being made available.
1. Communicate appropriate information, in an accessible manner, on the risks faced within a community after the conduct of a risk assessment.	
Operational Coordination	Establish and maintain a unified and coordinated operational structure and process that appropriately integrates all critical stakeholders and supports the execution of core capabilities.
1. Establish protocols to integrate mitigation data elements in support of operations within all states and territories and in coordination with Federal agencies.	
Community Resilience	Lead the integrated effort to recognize, understand, communicate, plan, and address risks so that the community can develop a set of actions to accomplish Mitigation and improve resilience.
1. Maximize the coverage of the U.S. population that has a localized, risk-informed mitigation plan developed through partnerships across the entire community.	

---

[14] The capability targets serve as strategic targets and will be vetted and refined, taking into consideration risk information and resource requirements, during the planning process established through PPD-8.

Mitigation Mission Area Capabilities and Preliminary Targets	
Long-term Vulnerability Reduction	Build and sustain resilient systems, communities, and critical infrastructure and key resources lifelines so as to reduce their vulnerability to natural, technological, and human-caused incidents by lessening the likelihood, severity, and duration of the adverse consequences related to these incidents.
1. Achieve a measurable decrease in the long-term vulnerability of the Nation against current baselines amid a growing population base and expanding infrastructure base.	
Risk and Disaster Resilience Assessment	Assess risk and disaster resilience so that decision makers, responders, and community members can take informed action to reduce their entity's risk and increase their resilience.
1. Ensure that states, territories, and the top 100 Metropolitan Statistical Areas (MSAs) complete a risk assessment that defines localized vulnerabilities and consequences associated with potential natural, technological, and human-caused threats and hazards to their natural, human, physical, cyber, and socioeconomic interests.	
Threats and Hazard Identification	Identify the threats and hazards that occur in the geographic area; determine the frequency and magnitude; and incorporate this into analysis and planning processes so as to clearly understand the needs of a community or entity.
1. Identify the threats and hazards within and across the states, territories, and the top 100 MSAs, in collaboration with the whole community, against a national standard based on sound science.	

Mission Area: Response

Response includes those capabilities necessary to save lives, protect property and the environment, and meet basic human needs after an incident has occurred. It is focused on ensuring that the Nation is able to effectively respond to any threat or hazard, including those with cascading effects, with an emphasis on saving and sustaining lives and stabilizing the incident, as well as rapidly meeting basic human needs, restoring basic services and community functionality, establishing a safe and secure environment, and supporting the transition to recovery.

Communities regularly deal with emergencies and disasters that have fewer impacts than those considered to be the greatest risk to the Nation. In addition, communities may have resident capacities to deal with the public's needs locally for many of these lesser incidents. Catastrophic incidents will require a much broader set of atypical partners to accomplish the capability targets for the Response core capabilities than those routinely addressed. Community involvement, therefore, is a vital link to providing additional support to response personnel and may often be the primary source of manpower in the first hours and days after a catastrophic incident. Because of this, community members should be encouraged to train, exercise, and partner with emergency management officials.

Given the scope and magnitude of a catastrophic incident involving cascading events, legal, policy, and regulatory waivers/exemptions/exceptions will be required to achieve many of the targets. These challenges should be identified during pre-incident planning to ensure they are accounted for during an incident.

Table 5: Response Mission Area Capabilities and Preliminary Targets[15]

Response Mission Area Capabilities and Preliminary Targets	
Planning	Conduct a systematic process engaging the whole community as appropriate in the development of executable strategic, operational, and/or community-based approaches to meet defined objectives.
1. Develop operational plans at the Federal level, and in the states and territories, that adequately identify critical objectives based on the planning requirement, provide a complete and integrated picture of the sequence and scope of the tasks to achieve the objectives, and are implementable within the time frame contemplated in the plan using available resources.	
Public Information and Warning	Deliver coordinated, prompt, reliable, and actionable information to the whole community through the use of clear, consistent, accessible, and culturally and linguistically appropriate methods to effectively relay information regarding any threat or hazard and, as appropriate, the actions being taken and the assistance being made available.
1. Inform all affected segments of society by all means necessary, including accessible tools, of critical lifesaving and life-sustaining information to expedite the delivery of emergency services and aid the public to take protective actions. 2. Deliver credible messages to inform ongoing emergency services and the public about protective measures and other life-sustaining actions and facilitate the transition to recovery.	
Operational Coordination	Establish and maintain a unified and coordinated operational structure and process that appropriately integrates all critical stakeholders and supports the execution of core capabilities.
1. Mobilize all critical resources and establish command, control, and coordination structures within the affected community and other coordinating bodies in surrounding communities and across the Nation and maintain as needed throughout the duration of an incident. 2. Enhance and maintain National Incident Management System (NIMS)-compliant command, control, and coordination structures to meet basic human needs, stabilize the incident, and transition to recovery.	
Critical Transportation	Provide transportation (including infrastructure access and accessible transportation services) for response priority objectives, including the evacuation of people and animals, and the delivery of vital response personnel, equipment, and services into the affected areas.
1. Establish physical access through appropriate transportation corridors and deliver required resources to save lives and to meet the needs of disaster survivors. 2. Ensure basic human needs are met, stabilize the incident, transition into recovery for an affected area, and restore basic services and community functionality.	

---

[15] The capability targets serve as strategic targets and will be vetted and refined, taking into consideration risk information and resource requirements, during the planning process established through PPD-8.

Response Mission Area Capabilities and Preliminary Targets	
Environmental Response/Health and Safety	Ensure the availability of guidance and resources to address all hazards including hazardous materials, acts of terrorism, and natural disasters in support of the responder operations and the affected communities.

1. Conduct health and safety hazard assessments and disseminate guidance and resources, to include deploying hazardous materials teams, to support environmental health and safety actions for response personnel and the affected population.
2. Assess, monitor, perform cleanup actions, and provide resources to meet resource requirements and to transition from sustained response to short-term recovery.

Fatality Management Services	Provide fatality management services, including body recovery and victim identification, working with state and local authorities to provide temporary mortuary solutions, sharing information with mass care services for the purpose of reunifying family members and caregivers with missing persons/remains, and providing counseling to the bereaved.

1. Establish and maintain operations to recover a significant number of fatalities over a geographically dispersed area.

Infrastructure Systems	Stabilize critical infrastructure functions, minimize health and safety threats, and efficiently restore and revitalize systems and services to support a viable, resilient community.

1. Decrease and stabilize immediate infrastructure threats to the affected population, to include survivors in the heavily-damaged zone, nearby communities that may be affected by cascading effects, and mass care support facilities and evacuation processing centers with a focus on life-sustainment and congregate care services.
2. Re-establish critical infrastructure within the affected areas to support ongoing emergency response operations, life sustainment, community functionality, and a transition to recovery.

Mass Care Services	Provide life-sustaining services to the affected population with a focus on hydration, feeding, and sheltering to those who have the most need, as well as support for reunifying families.

1. Move and deliver resources and capabilities to meet the needs of disaster survivors, including individuals with access and functional needs and others who may be considered to be at-risk.
2. Establish, staff, and equip emergency shelters and other temporary housing options (including accessible housing) for the affected population.
3. Move from congregate care to non-congregate care alternatives and provide relocation assistance or interim housing solutions for families unable to return to their pre-disaster homes.

Response Mission Area Capabilities and Preliminary Targets	
Mass Search and Rescue Operations	Deliver traditional and atypical search and rescue capabilities, including personnel, services, animals, and assets to survivors in need, with the goal of saving the greatest number of endangered lives in the shortest time possible.

1. Conduct search and rescue operations to locate and rescue persons in distress, based on the requirements of state and local authorities.
2. Initiate community-based search and rescue support operations across a wide geographically dispersed area.
3. Ensure the synchronized deployment of local, regional, national, and international teams to reinforce ongoing search and rescue efforts and transition to recovery.

On-scene Security and Protection	Ensure a safe and secure environment through law enforcement and related security and protection operations for people and communities located within affected areas and also for all traditional and atypical response personnel engaged in lifesaving and life-sustaining operations.

1. Establish a safe and secure environment in an affected area.
2. Provide and maintain on-scene security and meet the protection needs of the affected population over a geographically dispersed area while eliminating or mitigating the risk of further damage to persons, property, and the environment.

Operational Communications	Ensure the capacity for timely communications in support of security, situational awareness, and operations by any and all means available, among and between affected communities in the impact area and all response forces.

1. Ensure the capacity to communicate with both the emergency response community and the affected populations and establish interoperable voice and data communications between Federal, state, and local first responders.
2. Re-establish sufficient communications infrastructure within the affected areas to support ongoing life-sustaining activities, provide basic human needs, and transition to recovery.

Public and Private Services and Resources	Provide essential public and private services and resources to the affected population and surrounding communities, to include emergency power to critical facilities, fuel support for emergency responders, and access to community staples (e.g., grocery stores, pharmacies, and banks) and fire and other first response services.

1. Mobilize and deliver governmental, nongovernmental, and private sector resources within and outside of the affected area to save lives, sustain lives, meet basic human needs, stabilize the incident, and transition to recovery, to include moving and delivering resources and services to meet the needs of disaster survivors.
2. Enhance public and private resource and services support for an affected area.

Response Mission Area Capabilities and Preliminary Targets	
Public Health and Medical Services	Provide lifesaving medical treatment via emergency medical services and related operations and avoid additional disease and injury by providing targeted public health and medical support and products to all people in need within the affected area.

1. Deliver medical countermeasures to exposed populations.
2. Complete triage and initial stabilization of casualties and begin definitive care for those likely to survive their injuries.
3. Return medical surge resources to pre-incident levels, complete health assessments, and identify recovery processes.

Situational Assessment	Provide all decision makers with decision-relevant information regarding the nature and extent of the hazard, any cascading effects, and the status of the response.

1. Deliver information sufficient to inform decision making regarding immediate lifesaving and life-sustaining activities and engage governmental, private, and civic sector resources within and outside of the affected area to meet basic human needs and stabilize the incident.
2. Deliver enhanced information to reinforce ongoing lifesaving and life-sustaining activities, and engage governmental, private, and civic sector resources within and outside of the affected area to meet basic human needs, stabilize the incident, and transition to recovery.

Mission Area: Recovery

Recovery includes those capabilities necessary to assist communities affected by an incident in recovering effectively. It is focused on a timely restoration, strengthening, and revitalization of the infrastructure; housing; a sustainable economy; and the health, social, cultural, historic, and environmental fabric of communities affected by a catastrophic incident.

The ability of a community to accelerate the recovery process begins with its efforts in pre-disaster preparedness, including mitigation and planning for and building capacity for disaster recovery. These efforts result in a resilient community with an improved ability to withstand, respond to, and recover from disasters, which can significantly reduce recovery time and costs.

After an incident, recovery encompasses more than the restoration of a community's physical structures. Of equal importance is providing a continuum of care to support individuals in maintaining or restoring health, safety, and independence, and in meeting the needs of survivors and response and recovery personnel who experienced financial, emotional, and physical hardships while positioning the community to meet the needs of the future. Strengthening the health and social services, social fabric, accessibility, infrastructure, educational and child care systems, environmental sustainability, historic and cultural resources, and economic vitality serves to meet these needs and enhance the resiliency of the entire community as recovery progresses.

Successful recovery requires informed and coordinated leadership throughout the whole community during all phases of the recovery process. It also acknowledges the linkages between the recovery of individuals, families, and communities and addresses the full range of physical, programmatic, communications, psychological, and emotional needs of the community, including response and recovery personnel.

Partnerships and inclusiveness are vital for ensuring that all voices are heard and that available resources are coordinated in advance of a disaster, if possible, and contributed when needed. Everyone must have equal opportunity to participate in community recovery efforts in a meaningful way. Clear, consistent, accessible (including for those with limited English proficiency and individuals with disabilities), culturally appropriate, and effective communication initiatives are critical.

State and local governments play the lead role in planning for and managing all aspects of their jurisdiction's recovery and ensuring that key community organizations and individuals in community leadership roles are included. A successful recovery process requires unity of effort among resource providers and recovery managers, respecting the authority and expertise of each participating organization while coordinating the support of common recovery objectives.

Table 6: Recovery Mission Area Capabilities and Preliminary Targets[16]

Recovery Mission Area Capabilities and Preliminary Targets
Planning — Conduct a systematic process engaging the whole community as appropriate in the development of executable strategic, operational, and/or community-based approaches to meet defined objectives.
1. Convene the core of an inclusive planning team (identified pre-disaster), which will oversee disaster recovery planning.   2. Complete an initial recovery plan that provides an overall strategy and timeline, addresses all core capabilities, and integrates socioeconomic, demographic, accessibility, and risk assessment considerations, which will be implemented in accordance with the timeline contained in the plan.
Public Information and Warning — Deliver coordinated, prompt, reliable, and actionable information to the whole community through the use of clear, consistent, accessible, and culturally and linguistically appropriate methods to effectively relay information regarding any threat or hazard and, as appropriate, the actions being taken and the assistance being made available.
1. Reach all populations within the community with effective recovery-related public information messaging and communications that are accessible to people with disabilities and people with limited English proficiency, protect the health and safety of the affected population, help manage expectations, and ensure stakeholders have a clear understanding of available assistance and their roles and responsibilities.   2. Support affected populations and stakeholders with a system that provides appropriate, current information about any continued assistance, steady state resources for long-term impacts, and monitoring programs in an effective and accessible manner.

---

[16] The capability targets serve as strategic targets and will be vetted and refined, taking into consideration risk information and resource requirements, during the planning process established through PPD-8.

Recovery Mission Area Capabilities and Preliminary Targets	
Operational Coordination	Establish and maintain a unified and coordinated operational structure and process that appropriately integrates all critical stakeholders and supports the execution of core capabilities.

1. Establish tiered, integrated leadership, and inclusive coordinating organizations that operate with a unity of effort and are supported by sufficient assessment and analysis to provide defined structure and decision-making processes for recovery activities.
2. Define the path and timeline for recovery leadership to achieve the jurisdiction's objectives that effectively coordinates and uses appropriate Federal, state, and local assistance, as well as nongovernmental and private sector resources. This plan is to be implemented within the established timeline.

Economic Recovery	Return economic and business activities (including food and agriculture) to a healthy state and develop new business and employment opportunities that result in a sustainable and economically viable community.

1. Conduct a preliminary assessment of economic issues and identify potential inhibitors to fostering stabilization of the affected communities.
2. Ensure the community recovery and mitigation plan(s) incorporates economic revitalization and removes governmental inhibitors to post-disaster economic sustainability, while maintaining the civil rights of citizens.
3. Return affected areas to a sustainable economy within the specified time frame in the recovery plan.

Health and Social Services	Restore and improve health and social services networks to promote the resilience, independence, health (including behavioral health), and well-being of the whole community.

1. Restore basic health and social services functions. Identify critical areas of need for health and social services, as well as key partners and at-risk individuals (such as children, those with disabilities and others who have access and functional needs, and populations with limited English proficiency) in short-term, intermediate, and long-term recovery.
2. Complete an assessment of community health and social service needs and develop a comprehensive recovery timeline.
3. Restore and improve the resilience and sustainability of the health and social services networks to meet the needs of and promote the independence and well-being of community members in accordance with the specified recovery timeline.

Housing	Implement housing solutions that effectively support the needs of the whole community and contribute to its sustainability and resilience.

1. Assess preliminary housing impacts and needs, identify currently available options for temporary housing, and plan for permanent housing.
2. Ensure community housing recovery plans continue to address interim housing needs, assess options for permanent housing, and define a timeline for achieving a resilient, accessible, and sustainable housing market.
3. Establish a resilient and sustainable housing market that meets the needs of the community, including the need for accessible housing within the specified time frame in the recovery plan.

Recovery Mission Area Capabilities and Preliminary Targets	
Infrastructure Systems	Stabilize critical infrastructure functions, minimize health and safety threats, and efficiently restore and revitalize systems and services to support a viable, resilient community.

1. Restore and sustain essential services (public and private) to maintain community functionality.
2. Develop a plan with a specified timeline for redeveloping community infrastructures to contribute to resiliency, accessibility, and sustainability.
3. Provide systems that meet the community needs while minimizing service disruption during restoration within the specified timeline in the recovery plan.

Natural and Cultural Resources	Protect natural and cultural resources and historic properties through appropriate planning, mitigation, response, and recovery actions to preserve, conserve, rehabilitate, and restore them consistent with post-disaster community priorities and best practices and in compliance with appropriate environmental and historical preservation laws and executive orders.

1. Implement measures to protect and stabilize records and culturally significant documents, objects, and structures.
2. Mitigate the impacts to and stabilize the natural and cultural resources and conduct a preliminary assessment of the impacts that identifies protections that need to be in place during stabilization through recovery.
3. Complete an assessment of affected natural and cultural resources and develop a timeline for addressing these impacts in a sustainable and resilient manner.
4. Preserve natural and cultural resources as part of an overall community recovery that is achieved through the coordinated efforts of natural and cultural resource experts and the recovery team in accordance with the specified timeline in the recovery plan.

Conclusion and Next Steps

The Goal is designed to prepare our Nation for the risks that will severely tax our collective capabilities and resources. Each community contributes to the Goal by assessing and preparing for the risks that are most relevant and urgent for them individually, which in turn strengthens our collective security and resilience as a Nation. National preparedness will also be strengthened through collaboration and cooperation with international partners, including working closely with our neighbors Canada and Mexico, with whom we share common borders.

The anniversary of history's deadliest attack of international terrorism and a spate of natural disasters reminds us that America's security and resilience work is never finished. While we are safer, stronger, and better prepared than a decade ago, we remain resolute in our commitment to safeguard the Nation against the greatest risks it faces, now and for decades to come. This means the Goal is a living document, and it will be regularly reviewed to evaluate consistency with existing and new policies, evolving conditions, and the NIMS. The results of the first review will be submitted by November 1, 2012, and subsequent reviews will be conducted periodically in order to evaluate the Nation's progress toward building, sustaining, and delivering the core capabilities that are essential to a secure and resilient Nation.

The National Preparedness Goal is the cornerstone of implementation of PPD-8. In order to build, sustain, and deliver the core capabilities described in the National Preparedness Goal, several PPD-8 components will be implemented. These include:

- A National Preparedness System, which will describe and organize an integrated set of guidance, programs, and processes to enable the Nation to meet the Goal.

- A series of National Frameworks and Federal Interagency Operational Plans. The National Frameworks will address the roles and responsibilities across the whole community to deliver the core capabilities. The Federal Interagency Operational Plans will address the critical tasks, responsibilities, and resourcing, personnel, and sourcing requirements for the core capabilities.

- A National Preparedness Report, which will provide a summary of the progress being made toward building, sustaining, and delivering the core capabilities described in the Goal.

- A Campaign to Build and Sustain Preparedness, which will provide an integrating structure for new and existing community-based, nonprofit, and private sector preparedness programs, research and development activities, and preparedness assistance.

The results of these efforts and the specific deliverables called for in PPD-8 will inform current and future budget year planning and decisions. We will analyze current performance against our intended capabilities, the defined targets, and associated performance measures. This analysis will enable us to individually and collectively determine necessary resource levels, inform resource allocation plans, and guide Federal preparedness assistance. Budget implications across the preparedness enterprise cannot be assessed without this detailed and specific information. This approach will allow for annual adjustments based on updated priorities and our resource posture.

This page intentionally left blank.

Appendix A: Terms and Definitions

All-of-Nation: See Whole Community.

Capability Targets: The performance threshold(s) for each core capability.

Core Capabilities: Distinct critical elements necessary to achieve the National Preparedness Goal.

Critical Infrastructure: Systems and assets, whether physical or virtual, so vital to the United States that the incapacity or destruction of such systems and assets would have a debilitating impact on security, national economic security, national public health or safety, or any combination thereof. The Nation's critical infrastructure is composed of 18 sectors: banking and finance; chemical; commercial facilities; communications; critical manufacturing; dams; defense industrial base; emergency services; energy; food and agriculture; government facilities; healthcare and public health; information technology; national monuments and icons; nuclear reactors, material, and waste; postal and shipping; transportation systems; and water.

Cybersecurity: Encompasses the cyberspace global domain of operations consisting of the interdependent network of information technology infrastructures, and includes the Internet, telecommunications networks, computer systems, and embedded processors and controllers in critical industries. The cybersecurity core capability is the means for protecting cyberspace from damage, unauthorized use, or exploitation of electronic information and communications systems and the information contained therein to ensure confidentiality, integrity, and availability.

Imminent Threat: Intelligence or operational information that warns of a credible, specific, and impending terrorist threat or ongoing attack against the United States and its territories that is sufficiently specific and credible to recommend implementation of protective measures to thwart or mitigate against an attack.

Intelligence Cycle: The process of developing raw information into finished intelligence for policymakers, military commanders, law enforcement partners, and other consumers to use in making decisions. The cycle is highly dynamic and never ending. For the purposes of the National Prevention Framework, there are six steps in the intelligence cycle: planning and direction (establish the intelligence requirements of the consumer); collection (gather the raw data required to produce the desired finished product); processing and exploitation (convert the raw data into comprehensible form that is usable for producing the finished product); analysis and production (integrate, evaluate, analyze, and prepare the processed information for inclusion in the finished product); dissemination (deliver the finished product to the consumer who requested it and to others as applicable); and evaluation and feedback (acquire continual feedback during the cycle that aids in refining each individual stage and the cycle as a whole).

Mission Areas: Groups of core capabilities, including Prevention, Protection, Mitigation, Response, and Recovery.

Mitigation: The capabilities necessary to reduce loss of life and property by lessening the impact of disasters.

National Health Security: The Nation and its people are prepared for, protected from, and resilient in the face of health threats or hazards with potentially negative health consequences.

National Preparedness: The actions taken to plan, organize, equip, train, and exercise to build and sustain the capabilities necessary to prevent, protect against, mitigate the effects of, respond to, and recover from those threats that pose the greatest risk to the security of the Nation.

Performance Measure: The metrics used to ascertain actual performance against target levels identified for each core capability; by design, they are clear, objective, and quantifiable.

Prevention: The capabilities necessary to avoid, prevent, or stop a threatened or actual act of terrorism. For the purposes of the prevention framework called for in PPD-8, the term "prevention" refers to preventing imminent threats.

Protection: The capabilities necessary to secure the homeland against acts of terrorism and manmade or natural disasters.

Recovery: The capabilities necessary to assist communities affected by an incident to recover effectively.

Resilience: The ability to adapt to changing conditions and withstand and rapidly recover from disruption due to emergencies.

Response: The capabilities necessary to save lives, protect property and the environment, and meet basic human needs after an incident has occurred.

Risk Assessment: A product or process that collects information and assigns a value to risks for the purpose of informing priorities, developing or comparing courses of action, and informing decision making.

Security: The protection of the Nation and its people, vital interests, and way of life.

Stabilization: The process by which the immediate impacts of an incident on community systems are managed and contained.

Terrorism: Any activity that involves an act that is dangerous to human life or potentially destructive of critical infrastructure or key resources and is a violation of the criminal laws of the United States or of any state or other subdivision of the United States; and, appears to be intended to intimidate or coerce a civilian population, or to influence the policy of a government by intimidation or coercion, or to affect the conduct of a government by mass destruction, assassination, or kidnapping. (Note that although the definition of terrorism includes both domestic and international acts of terrorism, the scope of the planning system is the prevention and protection against acts of terrorism in the homeland.)

Weapon of Mass Destruction: Any destructive device; any weapon that is designed or intended to cause death or serious bodily injury through the release, dissemination, or impact of toxic or poisonous chemicals or their precursors; any weapon involving a biological agent, toxin, or vector; or any weapon that is designed to release radiation or radioactivity at a level dangerous to human life.

Whole Community: A focus on enabling the participation in national preparedness activities of a wider range of players from the private and nonprofit sectors, including nongovernmental organizations and the general public, in conjunction with the participation of Federal, state, and local governmental partners in order to foster better coordination and working relationships. Used interchangeably with "all-of-Nation."

www.ingramcontent.com/pod-product-compliance
Lightning Source LLC
Chambersburg PA
CBHW080806290526
45790CB00008B/3595